THE
TWELVE
STEPS
REVISITED

Choices

Choices

THE
TWELVE
STEPS
REVISITED

Ronald L. Rogers
Chandler Scott McMillin
Morris A. Hill

BANTAM BOOKS
NEW YORK · TORONTO · LONDON · SYDNEY · AUCKLAND

THE TWELVE STEPS REVISITED

A Bantam Book / January 1990

PRINTING HISTORY

*Originally published by Education & Training Institute
of Maryland, Inc., and Madrona Publishers*

Library of Congress Cataloging-in-Publication Data

Rogers, Ronald.
    The twelve steps revisited / Ronald L. Rogers, Chandler Scott
McMillin, Morris A. Hill.
      p.   cm.
    Reprint. Originally published: Seattle : Madrona Publishers,
c.1988.
    Bibliography: p.
    ISBN 0-553-34733-0
    1. Alcoholics—Rehabilitation—United States. 2. Alcoholism—
United States—Psychological aspects. 3. Alcoholics Anonymous.
I. McMillin, Chandler. II. Hill, Morris A. III. Title. IV. Title:
12 steps revisited.
HV5279.R63 1990
362.29'286'0973—dc20

89-6876
CIP

Published simultaneously in the United States and Canada

---

*Bantam Books are published by Bantam Books, a division of Bantam
Doubleday Dell Publishing Group, Inc. Its trademark, consisting of
the words "Bantam Books" and the protrayal of a rooster, is Registered
in U.S. Patent and Trademark Office and in other countries. Marca
Registrada. Bantam Books, 666 Fifth Avenue, New York, New York 10103.*

PRINTED IN THE UNITED STATES OF AMERICA

OPM   0 9 8 7 6 5 4 3 2 1

CONTENTS

◆ ◆ ◆

THE
TWELVE
STEPS
REVISITED

Chapter 1

THE DISEASE OF ALCOHOLISM

◆◆◆

Rarely have we seen a person fail who has thoroughly followed our path." This statement, which begins Chapter Five of the "Big Book" of Alcoholics Anonymous is just as true today as it was when it was first published in 1939, when AA membership numbered about one hundred. The challenge today, as it was in 1939, is how to ensure that the "path" is "thoroughly followed."

The following pages are our attempt to, in some small way, help you or enable you to help someone else along that glorious path to sobriety, health, and happiness.

In directly treating or supervising the treatment of thousands of hospitalized alcoholics we observed early on that three things or processes had to be accomplished by our patients in order for the recovery process to succeed. First, they had to "self-diagnose," second, they had to assume responsibility for the treatment of their disease, and third, they had to learn how to use the "Program" or Steps of Alcoholics Anonymous for continued long-term recovery. If any of these three processes were omitted our patient, in most cases, would relapse.

We found that the physiological or Chronic Disease Model of alcoholism was the easiest for the patients to use for self-diagnosis and self-responsibility. As time has passed, research has shown that this is the true model of alcoholism, a chronic physiological disease process that is genetically transmitted. Our patients are able to identify their symptoms with the chronic physiological disease model, and therefore self-diagnose. It is certainly easier for someone to understand that he or she is responsible for treating a physiological disease than a mental or moral illness. After all, we treat colds and flu and their assorted aches and pains all of our lives. Very few people run to the doctor with a runny nose. But our patients could get self-diagnosis and self-responsibility by the gallon, and still relapse without the use of the AA Program for continued long-term recovery.

If you have read the book *Alcoholics Anonymous* or the "Big Book," as it is sometimes referred to, you know that the Twelve Steps are the program of Alcoholics Anonymous. You know that the Twelve Steps have very little to do with a physiological disease. In fact, only the First Step says anything about alcohol. Many of you who have used these Steps as a program of recovery already understand how they apply to the physiological disease of alcoholism. But for a person with the disease who is sick enough to be

4

detoxified in a hospital, it is tough to make the connection between the AA Steps and the disease process.

We want to be very clear about one thing: We are not trying to rewrite the Twelve Steps, nor are we trying to reinterpret the Twelve Steps. The Program has been powerful enough to help over one million people recover from this potentially fatal disease. Eventually each and every person in the program of Alcoholics Anonymous must decide what those steps mean for him or her, and from what we have heard from our thousands of friends in AA, the program is slightly different for each person.

What we have tried to do in the following pages is relate the Twelve Steps, Step by Step, to recovery from a physiological, chronic disease process called alcoholism. We have done this to help newly recovering people use the Twelve Steps and participate in the program of Alcoholics Anonymous with all the fellowship and love that goes along with that participation. We also hope that families and friends of people with the disease of alcoholism may learn a little more about the disease, about Alcoholics Anonymous, and perhaps about the use of the Al-Anon Family Program. Lastly, we hope that this may help explain to some not-so-newly recovering people something about the disease and the Twelve Steps, just in case they may have missed it along the way.

Chapter 2

SOMETHING IS WRONG WITH MY DRINKING

◆ ◆ ◆

STEP ONE *We admitted we were powerless over alcohol—that our lives had become unmanageable.*

Obviously, no sane human being will go to any lengths to solve a problem unless he or she believes a problem exists. Any effective treatment of alcoholism *must* be based on the alcoholic's acknowledgement of his or her own illness.

That admission—of powerlessness and unmanageable lives—is the cornerstone of the Twelve Step Program. Without it, the alcoholic finds it nearly impossible to successfully use the remaining Steps.

Why?

First of all, he or she is probably still drinking. And nothing, but nothing, interferes with clear thought, good judgement, and powerful action more effectively than the cycle of intoxication and withdrawal.

Thus we have come to believe, along with most of

the recovering alcoholics we know, that any alcoholic's ability to restore sanity through the Twelve Steps is dependent on the recognition of the need for total abstinence. In this respect, it seems to us that various half-measures—such as substituting tranquilizers for alcohol, or alternating little "slips" with periods on the wagon—are about as destructive as continuous drunkenness.

Without abstinence, alcoholics may get a little "better," but they just don't seem to get "well."

Since the First Step happens to be the only one in which alcohol is even mentioned, the meaning is clear: the key to establishing the maintaining abstinence lies here.

Perhaps more than in any other model of alcoholism, the Disease Model views abstinence as a *prerequisite* for recovery. This is because the physiological processes associated with this disease are largely involuntary. In short, when the alcoholic's body comes into contact with alcohol or similar drugs, a disease process takes over and begins dictating the body's response.

By controlling the response, the disease effectively dictates the alcoholic's desire for, and use of, alcohol.

In other words, alcoholism *tells* the alcoholic when, where, how often, and how much to drink. It is alcoholism which eventually makes alcohol the only effective medicine for the drinker's stresses and strains. It is alcoholism which leads the alcoholic to elevate drinking above all other interests, and it is alcoholism which insists that the victim drink despite the problems drinking causes.

It is the progression of this illness that ultimately renders the drinker powerless over alcohol, making life unmanageable. And it is the ability to recognize and acknowledge this reality which motivates recovery.

Here's how we believe alcoholism creates this degree of powerlessness and unmanageability.

The Signs of Powerlessness
Tolerance

Alcoholics have long been known to be able to consume larger-than-normal amounts of alcohol without being obviously sedated. This is a sign of alcoholic tolerance.

In our society tolerance is more frequently seen as a social advantage than as a possible symptom of alcoholism. Indeed, it *is* an advantage for a drinker to be able to consume a considerable amount of alcohol over the course of an evening without getting as sleepy, stupid, or obnoxious as everyone else.

Most people regard this as an indication of superior will power or strength of character, and we're understandably more likely to be concerned about a drinker who *does* get drunk than about one who *doesn't*.

For most of history, medicine assumed that the

legendary high tolerance of the alcoholic was invariably the result of heavy drinking. But for most alcoholics, high tolerance appears relatively early in their drinking careers, and actually serves to encourage the use of increased amounts of alcohol.

If drinking doesn't interfere with your functioning, why *not* drink more? This tolerance effectively blinds alcoholics, and those around them, to the increases in the amount or the frequency of their drinking.

In fact, alcoholic tolerance most likely represents a complex adaptation of the brain and liver to alcohol, and these adaptations probably begin early in the disease process.

Like other facets of alcoholism, tolerance tends to change as the disease progresses. After years of "protection" from the usual sedative and intoxicating effects of excessive drinking, the alcoholic's tolerance may desert him, and he finds that he now experiences bouts of drunkenness, obvious to everyone around him, even though he may actually be drinking *less* than he had been a few years earlier.

As the alcoholic was powerless over the gift of increased tolerance, so is the alcoholic powerless over its disappearance.

Physical Dependence

The second sign of the progression of alcoholism is the appearance of withdrawal symptoms.

Like most aspects of this disease, withdrawal symptoms are mild at the beginning, and worsen as the illness progresses.

The earliest indications of physical dependence are insomnia, anxiety, irritability, and nausea, especially after eating. These the alcoholic routinely attributes to stress, a hangover, a cold, or "the flu."

Later on, anxiety may become paralyzing attacks of unspecified fear, which only a drink seems to relieve. Occasional insomnia may turn into chronic sleeplessness, for which alcohol is the only effective remedy.

Nausea may turn into a daily episode of vomiting, often on an empty stomach. Irritability becomes a virtually constant state, and is accompanied by a hand tremor which somebody may actually, at long last, identify as a symptom of alcoholism.

The practical effect of physical addiction is to change the alcoholic's motive for drinking. No longer is alcohol a social or recreational drug. First and foremost, it has become a *medicine*.

Alcohol works better, faster, and more effectively than any other medicine because the body has adapted to it. Though he or she has no way of knowing it, alcohol is so effective precisely *because* he or she has become an alcoholic.

It should be easy to see how withdrawal dictates the amount and frequency of drinking. Alcoholics tend to drink as much as it takes to quiet their withdrawal-agitated nervous systems. They balance this physiological need with the constraints of accepted drinking practices.

If drinking on the job means losing your job, you'll probably resist drinking at work.

But when you get off work, a drink will be your first priority. And as withdrawal worsens, "accepted drinking practices" will become irrelevant, and the physiological need for alcohol, all-consuming.

Loss of Control

For most alcoholics, the final, indisputable sign of powerlessness is obvious loss of control.

This generally appears in three key areas: *the amount, the time and place, and the duration of the episode.*

Suppose an alcoholic attends a party with the intention of having a few drinks. Instead, he drinks to a point which exceeds even *his* tolerance, and makes a drunken pass at his buddy's wife.

He didn't intend to get drunk. He may even have intended to avoid getting drunk. Nonetheless, get drunk he did. That is a sign of loss of control over the amount he drinks.

Suppose, on the other hand, as a result of the above episode and others like it, he promises his wife he will abstain completely for one month. But he finds life so miserable without alcohol that he sneaks it whenever he can, taking care that she not discover him. In order to make it through a Saturday at home with the family, he has to make several trips to the garage "to check the lawnmower," or a similar excuse. While there, he nips from his secret supply of vodka. Or perhaps he's stashed a bottle in the bathroom, to help him survive a quiet weekend at home with the kids.

That is a sign of loss of control over *the time and place* for drinking. The toilet tank is not generally thought of as a liquor cabinet in our society.

As another example, picture an alcoholic eagerly awaiting her husband's business trip.

"I'll just have a few on Thursday," she tells herself. "I'll get rid of everything before he gets home Friday night. He'll never guess a thing."

Instead, he finds her two days later, passed out on the living room couch, surrounded by bottles.

She didn't plan on that happening.

Because all the first hundred alcoholics in AA were "low-bottom" drunks, well advanced in the progression of the illness, all had experienced unmistakable evidence of loss of control. This is perhaps why they selected the term "powerless" to describe their relationship with alcohol.

We now believe that the origins of this powerlessness lie in physical adaptations which may begin years before the obvious symptoms of loss of control.

Alcoholic Blackouts

It's one thing to do something stupid, embarrassing, or dangerous while drunk.

12

It's quite another thing when you can't even remember doing it.

It is hard to argue that drinkers who don't remember what they did or said during drinking episodes were fully in control of their actions. Maybe they were—and maybe they weren't.

Sometimes we hear an alcoholic say, "So what if I was in a blackout? I was able to function, wasn't I?"

Which is like saying, "So what if I stepped in front of a bus? It missed me, didn't it?"

There are millions of blackout stories in AA, but one of the favorites concerns the woman who, three months sober, decided to attend a cocktail party with her husband. Dressed to the nines and carrying a casserole in a covered dish, she set out by herself in a taxi to join her husband at the party. On the way, she decided to stop off and have a couple at the local bar.

Some time later, she woke from a sound sleep in the lobby of an airport. Horrified, she asked a porter where she could catch a cab, thinking she would make some excuse to her husband for not showing up at the affair.

The porter answered her in a foreign language.

She'd flown to Paris.

The casserole, she reported, was cold.

Physiological Deterioration

If there is one thing that frightens alcoholics, it is the possibility of diseases such as liver cirrhosis. But this illness reflects only a small part of the physiological deterioration which accompanies alcoholism.

Alcoholism is involved, directly and indirectly, in more hospital admissions than any other factor. This involvement may not be obvious, however, because an alcoholic is frequently admitted to the hospital under a diagnosis other than alcoholism.

Don't be fooled. A significant percentage of heart attack victims are alcoholic. So are many of those admitted for ulcers, pancreatitis, gastritis, lung disease, and a variety of other illnesses.

Many brain-impaired residents of chronic-care facilities, those who may not be able to recall having breakfast that morning, got that way because of alcoholism.

As much as physical illness might frighten an alcoholic, the chances are that without treatment specifically for alcoholism, he or she will continue drinking *despite* any medical complications that arise.

Why? Because that is the nature of alcoholism. And it is another excellent example of the extent to which an alcoholic becomes powerless over the drug.

WHY LIFE BECOMES UNMANAGEABLE

The second part of the First Step has to do with life becoming unmanageable.

Like other diseases that affect the brain, alcoholism "creates" a number of psychosocial symptoms which appear as problems related to drinking.

These are many and varied. As the disease progresses, they accumulate.

In the early stages, alcoholics suffer relatively few problems caused by their use of alcohol, despite the fact that *they already have the disease.*

In later stages, it sometimes seems as if life itself is simply one alcohol-related problem after another.

But there is an interesting wrinkle here: alcoholics, along with their families, friends, physicians, and most everyone else, tend to mistake these *results* of alcoholism for its *causes.*

Suppose we look at an alcoholic in the disease's middle stages, experiencing loss of control. With some regularity (but by no means every time he drinks), he consumes more than he intends to. As a result, he arrives home from "happy hour" with a very noticeable "buzz," and his wife begins to find this offensive, and complains about it.

Now if this problem continues despite her complaints, she will assume that it represents some sort of conscious choice on her husband's part. It would never occur to her that her otherwise perfectly competent mate is having trouble predicting what he will do once he starts drinking.

It doesn't occur to the alcoholic, either. Like her, he believes that excessive drinking is largely a matter of giving in to temptation or lacking will power. He will, of course, resent what he perceives as her judgement that he is weak-willed or irresponsible. Unfortunately, there is no way to resolve this conflict.

Since the alcoholic is losing control over how much, how often, and how appropriately he drinks, he will continue, with increasing frequency, to drink more than his wife thinks he should.

Since she believes he is consciously disregarding her feelings, she will grow still more angry and hostile in her approach to him.

He will then come to believe that it is *her hostility* which pushes him toward alcohol. She will become convinced that he is personally responsible for her increasing anger. What is missing, of course, is any awareness of the disease process.

As this stalemate escalates into sexual incompatibility, arguments about parenting and money, and almost total breakdown in communication, it is easy to forget that these conflicts are really the result of untreated alcoholism. No alcoholism, no problem. Other problems, perhaps—but not these.

Five years later, after a painful divorce, this alcoholic turns up in treatment. From what point does he date his excessive drinking? Usually, from the last stages of his marriage. He forgets, or perhaps never understood, the role alcoholism played in the breakup of the marriage.

Because alcohol interferes with brain functioning, the alcoholic in the middle and later stages may find it increasingly difficult to manage aspects of life he might once have taken for granted. Trapped between intoxication and withdrawal, less and less able to drink without problems, he will suffer from alcoholism in every area of life.

In some respects, he suffers more—from guilt, worry, anxiety, mental confusion, self-doubt, and actual physical discomfort—when he *isn't* drinking than when he *is,* which further cements his belief that giving up alcohol would just about finish him off.

It isn't unusual for a counselor or doctor to encounter an alcoholic who is experiencing marital, legal, parental, financial, sexual, occupational, and emotional problems—*all at the same time*—all of which can be traced directly to alcoholic drinking.

It is often these problems that motivate an otherwise resistant alcoholic to seek help.

In most societies, people who have trouble managing their affairs tend to accumulate other people whose job it is to manage life *for* them. Such managers may include judges, doctors, probation officers, counselors, and clergy.

If you find that you have one or more of these managers in your life because of your drinking, that is an indicator of alcoholism.

◆

It's important to remember that in the Disease Model, powerlessness and unmanageability are understood as the logical outcome of the progression of alcoholism. They represent nothing more than an altered physiological state, and its long-term effect on the alcoholic's behavior.

In a similar but perhaps less dramatic way, victims of diabetes, heart disease, and emphysema experience a form of powerlessness over certain aspects of their existence.

An emphysemic doesn't plan on getting emphysema, but still has to accept diminished lung capacity, and learn to live with a bit less air.

A heart patient may not have known his heart was weakening over the years, but once he is told, he has to accept the necessity of cutting back on work and stress.

A diabetic doesn't like to give herself daily injections, but knows that without them she might not survive her intake of sugar.

In each instance, effective treatment depends on the individual's willingness to admit the extent and severity of his or her disease, and acknowledge the importance of treating it.

In the same way, alcoholics learn to live without alcohol—which is not easy for most of them—*simply because they have to.*

It is necessary because they have become powerless over alcohol, and life has grown unmanageable.

Chapter 3

SHOW ME THE WAY OUT

◆ ◆ ◆

STEP TWO *Came to believe that a Power greater than ourselves could restore us to sanity.*

To understand Step Two, put yourself in the place of an early AA member, before the Big Book was written, even before the organization got its name.

If you were typical of that group, you had during your lifetime made tens of thousands of promises to stop drinking, to hundreds of different people. Sometimes, you kept your promise for a few months. Sometimes, you broke it within the hour.

You might well have already sacrificed your job, fortune, or family in your pursuit of the ability to drink. In fact, you may have done so several times over.

After years of stubborn insistence of doing things your way, you had finally, reluctantly, come to the conclusion that you were powerless over alcohol, and that your life was unmanageable. But then you found yourself faced with a new dilemma: if *you* were powerless, unable to recover through your own will, then who or what would provide you with the strength to learn to live without alcohol?

To give you, in effect, precisely that thing you had failed to find so many times in the past?

Obviously, the answer must lie outside yourself.

Here was born the concept of the Higher Power (also known as the HP).

Yes, the Higher Power is a "spiritual" concept. But it survived to meet a very practical need of the recovering alcoholic. It answered the question: Who will give me the strength to do what has to be done?

As most people know, "religion" and "spirituality" are not the same thing. Religion is simply a form that spiritual belief may take. The fact that there exists a multitude of religions is evidence that spiritual belief can and does take many forms.

Spirituality, however, transcends these forms. Spiritually strong people may be Catholic, Protestant, Jewish, Muslim, or whatever. They may be members of no organized church at all.

Recall that early in its existence, AA realized that its purpose was not to *exclude* suffering alcoholics because of religion, but rather to *include* as many as possible. Thus the Steps, like the rest of the AA Program, are *not* geared to a particular religion.

And in fact, there are probably as many Higher Powers in AA as there are alcoholics.

Because a lot of people in AA have strong religious backgrounds, there are those for whom the Higher Power must be God, in one form or another.

Because there are also a number of agnostics and atheists in AA, it is common to find something other than God used as a Higher Power.

For example, many AA's use their Home Group as a Higher Power. They tell us that they believe the Higher Power expresses itself best through the actions of the group. By practicing the Twelve Steps, they maintain, their spiritual program is as strong as anyone's. Later on, we'll tell you a story about an alcoholic whose Higher Power was an inanimate object.

The important point: *the Higher Power must never be the alcoholic*. We already know *that* doesn't work.

◆

Notice that the Step employs the word "could" rather than "would" in describing what the Higher Power can do for the alcoholic.

Wouldn't it be great if all you needed was to believe in a power greater than yourself, and your sanity would automatically be restored?

You'd never have to worry about fooling yourself into having "just one little drink." You'd know what decision to make in a crisis. You'd be free of craving. You'd be serene, content with your lot, happy with yourself.

And you'd be able to skip the rest of the Steps.

Unfortunately, it doesn't work that way. Though the Second Step asserts that something exists which *can* restore your sanity, it doesn't promise that it *will*.

Instead, the Step offers a sort of "contract" between the HP and the suffering alcoholic. It proposes a *working relationship* along the lines of: "If you do this, then you will have the strength to do something else."

What does the alcoholic have to do to fulfill his or her part of the bargain?

Remain abstinent, one day at a time if necessary.

Attend meetings.

And begin working the Third Step.

◆

Apart from the issue of the Higher Power, the most discussed part of the Second Step has to do with "sanity."

Are alcoholics, it is frequently asked, really "insane"?

Yes and no.

For the most part, alcoholics are *not* mentally disturbed in the same sense that a schizophrenic or a manic-depressive person might be. Though it is not uncommon to encounter alcoholics who also suffer from chronic mental illness, the vast majority do not.

And further, recent research persuades us that far from drinking to "cover up" or self-medicate an underlying mental or emotional disturbance, the alcoholic experiences depressions, mood swings, personality problems, and general "craziness" *because* of alcoholism and the experience of alcoholic drinking.

There is strong evidence, obtained from studies that span decades in the lives of their subjects, that alcoholics show no special incidence of personality or psychological disorder prior to the onset of their alcoholism.

There is, however, one type of insanity that alcoholics share with just about everyone who suffers from addiction or from certain other chronic diseases. This particular form of craziness is often as dangerous to the health and happiness of the victim as schizophrenia is to its victims.

The "insanity" we refer to is evidenced by behavior such as:

Drinking despite knowing it will bring you trouble.

Drinking despite the pain and discontent it brings those you care about.

Drinking despite the damage you know it is doing to your health.

Drinking "at" someone who has offended you.

Drinking to prove you can handle it, despite your experience that you can't.

Cutting off friends, family, and whoever else interferes with your drinking.

Blaming other people for the fact that you can't drink safely.

23

Insisting, despite all evidence to the contrary, that you are "different" from other people who have alcoholism.

Making excuses for relapse after you have managed to abstain for awhile.

Resisting the efforts of those around you to get you to seek the help you need.

Letting your pride stand in the way of accepting treatment.

All addicts share this type of "insanity," and for them, it is every bit as dangerous as an actual brain disease.

Like a diabetic who refuses insulin, or a heart patient who insists on working sixteen hours a day, an alcoholic who is in the grip of this irrationality will actually *fight* getting well. And believe us, this can be a "fight to the death." If that isn't insanity, we don't know what is.

Chapter 4

LEARNING TO
FOLLOW DIRECTIONS

◆◆◆

STEP THREE *Made a decision to turn our will and our lives over to the care of God* as we understood Him.

I n the First Step, you recall, the alcoholics admitted that they suffered from alcoholism, a progressive disease which robbed them of their power over alcohol and rendered their lives unmanageable.

This admission provided the motivation to work the remaining Steps.

In Step Two, alcoholics chose a power greater than themselves to give them strength and guidance along the road to recovery. Thus the Second Step provided what will power could not.

Notice that so far, despite these changes in attitude and approach, a suffering alcoholic hasn't really been required to *do* anything. He or she has taken no specific *action*, made no actual alterations in lifestyle, outside (presumably) of quitting drinking, and attending a few meetings.

Sounds too easy to be true. It is.

The real changes begin with the Third Step. This is sometimes called the "action Step."

It has also been called the "most difficult" Step, and even the Step that "separates the winners from the losers." To understand why, and to grasp the importance of the Third Step in the Twelve Step Program, we should introduce the humble concept of "following directions." That phrase is encountered throughout AA, and for good reason. It may actually be the *key* to the initial months of involvement.

Most people, alcoholics included, are not really very good at following directions. We all know individuals who, when they get a Christmas present that specifies "some assembly required," insist on tinkering about for an hour or two *before* they look around for the directions they were supposed to follow in the first place. By that time, of course, the present is an unrecognizable mess.

Most of us know people who regard it as a personal insult to be expected to seek guidance in anything they attempt. These are the folks who wander around strange neighborhoods in the dead of night rather than ask directions at a local service station. And no less common are people who appear to respond only to "reverse motivation"—to get them to do something, you need only tell them *not* to do it.

This usually harmless trait becomes dangerous when applied to life-threatening diseases, because survival for victims of such illnesses may depend solely on their ability and willingness to follow certain directions.

We have no cure for alcoholism. As far as we can tell, an alcoholic remains alcoholic from the day he or she is diagnosed to the day life itself ends. Very little choice is involved in this. The alcoholic's only real choice is whether to be a *drinking* or a *sober* alcoholic.

Therefore, the goal in alcoholism treatment is not to cure, but rather to *arrest* the disease: to shift it from its active, dangerous phase, to a dormant phase. That happens when the alcoholic stops drinking, detoxifies, and begins the process of recovery.

Then the goal becomes teaching the alcoholic to *keep* the illness in the dormant phase, through the use of simple but effective treatments. These treatments are administered not by the doctor or the counselor, but by the patient himself.

Exactly the same situation develops with some forms of diabetes. Once the blood sugar is stabilized, the diabetic is given a diet, a supply of insulin to inject daily, and a kit for monitoring blood sugar. If the patient follows these directions, he or she has a good chance of establishing a happy, healthy, productive lifestyle—despite having diabetes.

Nobody takes diabetics aside and asks them if they like following these instructions. The fact is, most diabetics do not like it at all. They go through a period of resisting the regimen. They experiment, in some cases, with clever methods of cheating on their diets, and the like.

If the diabetic goes a little too far with this cheating, however, or fails to monitor the blood sugar adequately, the disease sends a little "message," in the form of a fainting spell or perhaps something much more serious. The person is still a diabetic and cannot forget it.

Like the diabetic, the alcoholic is handed directions to follow, by AA and by medical science, and is assured that these instructions will make it possible to live peacefully with the disease.

But in the course of following these directions, the alcoholic frequently finds himself in the position of having to do something he or she does not particularly *want* to do. Like giving up friends that he would rather keep, simply because their own drinking practices would threaten his sobriety. Like skipping a Caribbean cruise she's always wanted to take, because her sponsor tells her that it's too risky for her tender sobriety. Like swallowing his pride, relinquishing a favorite resentment, giving up something he wants. This is where resistance sets in. "Sure, I'll give up the booze," she insists, "but I don't see why I have to do this *other* stuff."

The Third Step is in fact a direct acknowledgement of the alcoholic's need to make a conscious decision to follow certain directions. It implies that you are willing to follow those directions you *don't* particularly like, as well as those you *do*.

It's as simple as this: because you found yourself powerless over this disease, you looked outside yourself for help, and identified a Higher Power that you believed could lead you to sanity. Now you have to turn your will and life over to that Power. After all, what good is a Higher Power if you don't use it? And what good were the first two Steps, without taking the Third?

Answer: not much good at all.

Perhaps you can see why this Step is so crucial, and yet so difficult, for some alcoholics. It involves not only living your life differently, but also allowing other people to give you directions which you then follow, even if they're sometimes contrary to your own desires or convenience.

In any randomly selected group of fifty people, there will probably be a few individuals who are good at following directions. Then there will be a larger group who are sometimes good, sometimes bad, depending on the phase of the moon. Finally, there will be a very large group of people who just flat-out hate to be told what to do, or to have to take actions they don't like.

Which segment do you think has the most trouble with recovery, whether from alcoholism, diabetes, or heart disease?

You guessed it.

Oddly enough, some people think that the important phrase in this Step is "God as we understood Him." We disagree. We believe the key to this Step lies in grasping what it means to "turn your will and life over." It's our impression that the phrase *"as we understood Him"* is emphasized precisely because it doesn't really matter, in taking this Step, who or what you believe God to be. This further underscores the *spiritual* (rather than religious) nature of the Program itself.

If you have found a Higher Power you believe in, and you begin to turn your will and life over to that Power, then the Step should work for you.

We promised to tell a story about an alcoholic whose HP was an inanimate object. Here it is.

We knew a fellow whose job involved driving around all day in his truck, going from job site to job site. He was having a terrible time with the Second and Third Steps, because he couldn't bring himself to believe in any type of Higher Power, let alone turn things over to one. But he was afflicted with a million problems, about which he worried constantly while he drove around in his truck.

His sponsor suggested that since he couldn't bring himself to let go of these anxieties, he simply follow this procedure: Each time one of these problems occurred to him while he was driving, he was to pull over, write the problem down on a piece of notepaper, and stuff it in the glove compartment. That encouraged him to let go of that particular problem, for a little while at least.

Several months later, when his glove compartment had been filled and emptied eight or nine times, he came to the stunning realization that he had in fact been "turning things over" all along—and that his

Higher Power was the glove compartment of his truck.

It really doesn't matter what or who your HP might be. It only matters that you learn to *use* it.

Chapter **5**

THE SEARCH
FOR SELF-KNOWLEDGE

◆ ◆ ◆

STEP FOUR   *Made a searching and fearless moral inventory of ourselves.*

W ith alcoholism, as with other chronic diseases, the responsibility for success or failure in treatment rests squarely on the shoulders of the patient. Only the alcoholic can, with proper support and guidance, establish and maintain a program of recovery.

Therefore, the most effective way to treat this illness doesn't involve "helping" the alcoholic. It centers instead on teaching the alcoholic to help himself or herself. And the best foundation for "self-help" is *self-knowledge*. The better you know yourself, the better you are able to develop strategies for your recovery which actually work.

The Fourth Step promotes self-knowledge through a process of *self-examination*. By taking a long, hard look at yourself—your attitudes, actions, and behavior—you can identify strengths and weaknesses in your own program of recovery.

It is important to understand the use of the term "moral" in this Step. Moral issues are those that concern "right and wrong." The purpose of the Fourth Step isn't to point an accusatory finger at you, or at other people, for what has gone wrong in your life up to this moment. It does *not* exist to make you feel guilty about what you did or didn't do in the past.

The Fourth Step's primary value, we believe, lies in helping you identify those aspects of your behavior which might interfere with recovery. Such interference usually comes from two areas: *defenses* which blind you to the extent and severity of the illness, or to the dangers of relapse; and *unproductive irrational beliefs* which make life difficult, even when sober.

Although we'd be the first to argue against the suggestion that alcoholism represents any form of moral turpitude, or that the alcoholic is responsible for contracting the disease, we do believe there is a definite "moral" aspect to treatment. And that is: once you've understood what alcoholism is, and been diagnosed as an alcoholic, you are thereby obligated to *treat* it. And where treatment is concerned, there very definitely exist "right and wrong" ways to recover.

After years of working with alcoholics, we have come to believe that most alcoholics *do* want to recover from alcoholism, once they realize they suffer from it. In some cases, however, this desire to "be well" is undermined by defenses and irrational beliefs that predispose that alcoholic to failure. Thus we think the Fourth Step should be an assessment *by the alcoholic* of his or her own past behavior, present actions, and future plans, as regards this disease.

DEFENSES

Alcoholic defenses usually center around two types of behavior which in terms of this disease are most emphatically "wrong."

One is *drinking*. This isn't to say that the use of alcohol is innately wrong for most people—it isn't. But drinking *is* destructive to the alcoholic, and on some level, he or she knows this throughout the course of the disease. Drinking alcohol must somehow be justified *despite* the unpleasant consequences it brings. As the alcoholic loses control, and life becomes "unmanageable," these justifications become increasingly outlandish.

The second behavior, usually surrounded by a wall of defenses, involves *failure to develop an effective program for recovery*. Thus many alcoholics attempt to treat alcoholism by attending an occasional AA meeting, "dropping in" on a psychiatrist, or "drinking less." This is like trying to kill a bear with a fly swatter.

The following is a brief review of common alcoholic defenses. Note how each blinds the alcoholic to flaws in his or her own plan for treatment.

DENIAL is the traditional favorite of alcoholics everywhere; depending on the situation, it might appear as "No matter what anybody says, I do *not* have a drinking problem!" or as "Look, I quit drinking— I do *not* need AA anymore!" The alcoholic in denial simply refuses to admit the possibility that a problem exists, despite evidence to the contrary.

RATIONALIZATION allows the alcoholic to "excuse" the abnormal features of his use of alcohol through "unreasonable reasons." He might insist to his wife that the reason he got drunk at their dinner party was because he had been working too hard lately—ignoring the fact, let's say, that he also gets drunk when he *isn't* working particularly hard.

EXTERNALIZING involves blaming your drinking on forces outside yourself—such as job, spouse, kids, parents, childhood training, and so forth. An externalization like "You'd drink too, if you were married to (him, her, it)" may become, with the passage of time, "You'd drink too, if your mate had deserted you!"

MINIMIZING is another favorite, since it permits the alcoholic to acknowledge the existence of a problem

35

without admitting that it is interfering with his life. For example: "I drink, but not that much," or "I yell at my wife, but I never hit her."

INTELLECTUALIZING is what keeps so many otherwise intelligent alcoholics soused for a lifetime. These drinkers use lengthy philosophical arguments or picayune disputes to distract from the larger issue. An intellectualizer will acknowledge a "drinking problem," but wants to argue about whether or not alcoholism is really a disease. Lost in the shuffle is the fact that, disease or not, the drinker has once again avoided doing anything about it.

◆

And so on and so forth. Defenses such as these not only contribute to relapse, but also blind the alcoholic to the fact that relapse is on the way.

UNPRODUCTIVE IRRATIONAL BELIEFS

We all have a number of unproductive irrational beliefs which interfere with living even when we're sober. Some examples:

1. "Life has to be fair to me."
2. "I'm not like all those other people who have a drinking problem."

3. "Other people should live up to my standards."
4. "Life should be more exciting—I'm bored."
5. "I'll never, ever be able to forgive (forget) that."

Most of us, confronted with these ideas in black and white, willingly admit that they are unproductive, even absurd. Nonetheless, we act as though they are true.

Think of the woman who cries at the "unfairness" of discovering she is an alcoholic. "Why me?" she asks. To which the only answer is, "Why *not* you?"

Is it fair that some people develop cancer, diabetes, schizophrenia, heart disease? Is this somehow their *fault*? Fairness is a notion popular among human beings, but one which Mother Nature apparently has difficulty grasping.

Alcoholism isn't fair, but it does exist, and certain people "get it."

Consider the alcoholic who sits at an AA meeting thinking to himself, "Aha! That never happened to me! I'm not like these people," ignoring the fact that for every difference, he has *two* things in common with them, including the reason he has attended the meeting in the first place.

How difficult it will be for this alcoholic to accept the support and guidance of others. And an alcoholic (or anyone else, for that matter) who insists that other people live up to his standards is destined for a life of frustration and disappointment. Those "other people" have *their own* standards and agendas, and they are most stubborn about adhering to them.

We once heard a noted psychologist state that "people who are always bored are usually those who expect life to entertain them." It has always puzzled us when we hear alcoholics claim that sobriety is "dull," or that AA meetings are boring.

We were under the impression that AA was for those who wanted to stop drinking. *Movies* are for entertainment.

And last but not least, there are those who are given to holding resentments. Of all the dangers of sobriety, this may be the worst.

A "resentment," by the way, is not simply anger. It is anger about a situation in which you felt victimized, insulted, taken advantage of, or prejudiced against. Resentments harken back to the illusion that "life is fair," and make the simple admonition to "live one day at a time" an impossibility. How can you stay in the present, when you act as though life is controlled by the past?

Example: "She ran away five years ago. That's why I drink."

Sure. The best remedy for grief is to give yourself a case of liver cirrhosis.

Or how about: "I can't go to AA. I had a bad experience when I went a couple of years ago."

Obviously, it makes no sense to condemn an organization of a million people because of your experience with *one* of its members, whom you may never meet again.

The Fourth Step is, of course, taken in a slightly different way by every alcoholic who attempts it. And a reminder—the Fourth Step alone is of little use. It becomes truly valuable when combined with the Fifth Step.

Chapter **6**

FEEDBACK

◆ ◆ ◆

STEP FIVE *Admitted to God, to ourselves, and to another human being the exact nature of our wrongs.*

I f you have in your Fourth Step been to any extent "fearless and searching," you will have undoubtedly learned quite a bit about the way you operate.

In examining your past behavior for defense mechanisms, you no doubt found evidence of denial, rationalization, minimizing, and the rest, in places where you least expected. We're sure you've encountered some of the irrational beliefs we listed, along with similar illusions of your own invention.

The quality of your inventory will of course depend greatly on your intellectual and emotional state when you attempt it. A Fourth Step done at six weeks sober is very different from one completed by the same person at six months in the Program.

Why?

Simply because *you* have changed, and your psychological functioning improves with the passage of time, provided you do not actively harass your brain with alcohol or other drugs. That's why we call it "recovery."

In finishing a Fourth Step (no matter what your state of mind), you perform two valuable tasks which assist you in getting well.

First, you focus your attention, at long last, on *yourself*—most especially, on your *drinking*.

If you are like most alcoholics, this is in contrast to your attitude prior to entering AA. Then, your attention was usually focussed on everyone and everything *but* your drinking.

Secondly, the Fourth Step allows you to assess, to the best of your ability, the relative strengths and weaknesses of your own program, in view of the realities of treating alcoholism.

Here's an example. We knew a man who had been in and out of AA (or as it's often called, "around" the Program), for about a year. He attended meetings regularly, and seemed to want to succeed, but kept having relapses of about a week's duration every three months. Each relapse was, of course, more painful than the last, and even though he drank only for a few weeks during the year, he seemed to be accumulating more alcohol-related problems than when he drank daily.

At the urging of his sponsor, he went ahead and attempted a Fourth Step. Sure enough, he was able to identify the problem.

He had married, it turned out, into a large Italian family which loved to hold festive, wine-soaked parties at the slightest occasion. He and his wife always attended these parties, because they really liked her relatives, and didn't want to offend them.

Though our alcoholic friend was able to avoid drinking at the parties, he found, upon closer examination, that his "slips" usually occurred a week or two *after* one of these celebrations. He would find himself getting mildly unhappy, feeling sorry for himself, and angry at the idea of having to go to AA meetings.

"I would start to feel like it was unfair that I had to be such a fanatic about AA just to stay sober. Then I'd think, you know, I never drank as much as some of my wife's relatives do. Why don't *they* ever get into trouble? Why was it just me?

"And then I would think: If I tell those people at AA what I'm thinking, they'll just tell me to stop going to the parties. Well, they have no right to insist on that! I am *not* going to give up my family just because some alcoholic tells me to! This AA is for the birds! It's like being in the Hitler youth! Well, I'm standing up for myself, and I'm not going to let a bunch of drunks push me around!"

Inevitably, he'd get drunk a couple of days later. His Fourth Step showed him the problem: attending those parties brought out every scrap of resentment and self-pity he had.

Another thing which a lot of people discover in the Fourth Step is that they have been putting the responsibility for their behavior onto other people, often for years.

A man might find that he has been punishing his wife for most of their marriage for "causing" his desire to drink. Each time he got into trouble with alcohol, he'd blame it on her "coldness," "nagging," or similar imperfections. She became the "bitch" he complained about to anyone who would listen—usually while he was sitting on a bar stool. Then during treatment, he learns to his horror that alcoholism is a disease, and that his drinking was not her fault.

As a result, he also realizes that in addition to suffering from his *drinking,* she has suffered as well from his blaming his drinking on her.

Now he sees the problem: along with being an alcoholic, he has been an externalizer, a "blamer." He has acted for years as though other people were *forcing* him to drink. But now his question is: Can she ever forgive me? Doesn't my wife *hate* me by now?

In the past, sudden awareness of his own self-deception, and the accompanying guilt, would have immediately been treated with more alcohol. He's decided not to do that now; he's learned it doesn't solve anything.

So here he sits, in possession of something resembling the "truth" about himself and his past behavior. He's seen, through the Fourth Step, not only his own defenses at work, but also the damage they can do. What does he do with this new self-knowledge? How does he live with it, make productive use of it?

43

Through the Fifth Step. Which in fact consists of *three separate admissions*.

The first is to God. We already discussed that "God" may be whatever Higher Power you choose. If your Higher Power is your AA group, then you may choose to admit your "wrongs" to members of that group.

The second is to yourself. You are being asked to learn to call a spade a spade. Don't sugar-coat issues. If you treated your mate or your kids badly while you were drinking, *then say that,* in just those words.

The point, after all, is to grasp the reality of alcoholism, in all its severity, and in the wide range of adverse consequences it has inflicted upon your life.

It is through this reality that you accept the existence of the disease, and become comfortable with the need to treat it.

The third admission is to another human being. We suggest that you select someone to whom you believe you will tell the truth. That may be a close friend, probably in AA, whom you admire, respect, and trust. It might be a virtual stranger. Whichever, it should be someone from whom you will accept feedback.

Most people in AA use their sponsor for their Fifth Step. If you have no sponsor, go back to the Fourth Step and see if you can discover why.

Perhaps you're putting off the commitment involved in the sponsor-newcomer relationship. Perhaps you're looking for a "guru" rather than a sponsor. Perhaps you're being egotistical, believing that no one can teach you anything.

An important benefit of the Fifth Step is that it burns some key bridges between you and that old, sick, defense-ridden alcoholic self you were. It will of course be difficult for you to return to your old alibis after heightening both your awareness and that of others who know you.

The Fifth Step, in this way, closes one door—to the past—while opening a new one—to the present. You are now engaged in active dialogue with your Higher Power, another person, and most importantly, yourself.

This reinforces your image of yourself not only as an alcoholic, but most importantly, as an alcoholic who is getting *well*.

Psychologists love to talk about the alcoholic's "low self esteem." The Twelve Steps will remedy that, if you allow them.

Chapter 7

NEEDING TO CHANGE, AND CHANGING

◆ ◆ ◆

STEP SIX   *Were entirely ready to have God remove all these defects of character.*

STEP SEVEN   *Humbly asked Him to remove our shortcomings.*

Since Steps Six and Seven are virtually inseparable in practice, we'll discuss them together.

But in order to show how these two Steps can be used in recovery, we need to clarify the phrase "defects of character" in Step Six.

Understand, first of all, that for most of history, alcoholism has been wrongly identified as a personality disorder. This misidentification was so pervasive that nearly everyone, alcoholic and non-alcoholic alike, grew up with the belief that alcoholics drank excessively because of moral or psychological weakness.

This is really a great injustice to the alcoholic.

In the first place, it isn't true. The concept of alcoholism as a character disorder simply doesn't fit the facts as we now know them.

More significantly, this misconception stigmatized the alcoholic, in the way epilepsy once stigmatized its victims.

Perhaps more than any other factor, this stigma has prevented alcoholics from seeking treatment, and has resulted in the unnecessary deaths of thousands of them, despite the fact that alcoholism is treatable.

How does stigmatizing interfere?

By turning the name of a disease into a nasty word, and a diagnosis into an accusation.

By pinning alcoholic drinking on vague personality "defects," which further separate the already isolated alcoholic from the human race.

By teaching those around the alcoholic to misinterpret his behavior, and by teaching the alcoholic to misunderstand himself.

That's what we think the idea of an "alcoholic personality disorder" has done to the alcoholic.

So you can see why we take such pains to explain what we believe is the proper interpretation of the term "defects of character." All too often, well-meaning people use that phrase as a justification for returning to the old-fashioned, pre-Disease Model, character-disorder theory.

It's our belief that "defects of character" should refer to the kind of defense mechanisms and irrational ideas that we discussed in the chapter on Step

Four. Because it is those aspects of the alcoholic's "character" which actually have to be dealt with in recovery.

In the Fourth Step, the alcoholic identified attitudes, beliefs, and behavior which had caused problems in the past.

In the Fifth Step, this self-assessment was shared with a new-found Higher Power and with another person.

Now, the Steps imply, the alcoholic must begin the long process of *changing* those attitudes and behaviors.

Why? Simply because without such changes, sobriety remains fragile, and "serenity" an impossibility.

In AA, serenity is usually seen as a by-product of acceptance—of your illness and the need to treat it; of yourself as you are at this moment; and of the world as you find it, with all its imperfections.

This kind of acceptance obviously can't be achieved simply by wishing for it—it represents ongoing use of the AA Program over the course of time.

Nevertheless, the first move toward acceptance comes through the Sixth and Seventh Steps, with their emphasis on changing attitudes.

Notice that change is portrayed as requiring not one but *two* separate actions.

The first is the assumption of a position of *readiness*. The alcoholic *prepares* himself or herself for change.

48

You don't just say, "OK, HP, I'm changing everything about myself now, so don't worry, this is a new person you've got here, everything's gonna be different from here on out."

Changing yourself isn't like changing your socks. And being *ready* for change isn't the same thing as wishing for it.

Consider a woman we know who had tried for years to give up smoking. Each attempt would last for a few weeks, and then she'd relapse. She visited hypnotists, clinics, and everyone else she could think of, but always met with failure. Finally, she just gave up.

"To hell with it," she thought. "I know I'll probably die of lung cancer, but I guess I don't care. I certainly don't seem to be able to muster the will power to quit smoking."

About three months after she'd made this decision, in the middle of a normal three-pack day, she read an article in a magazine about nicotine addiction. She'd never encountered this concept before, she'd always viewed smoking as a bad habit, or a response to stress, and her previous treatment had reinforced this. It had never occurred to her that she might smoke so much, and so persistently, because she was physically addicted to a drug.

But this made a lot of sense to her. She could understand how will power might fail when pitted against the pain of withdrawal. She could see the source of her feeling that she absolutely had to smoke every few minutes.

And she also perceived the shining truth that if her discomfort, anxiety, sleeplessness, and irritability were products of a withdrawal syndrome, they would have to fade away with time. Everyone knew that withdrawal couldn't last forever.

An idea began to germinate in her mind. "Maybe," she thought, "the reason I start smoking again after treatment is because I convince myself that my discomfort will never go away! Maybe I expect more from my body than is reasonable — such as to lose this craving for nicotine after only three weeks.

"If, on the other hand, I knew the craving and the discomfort would lessen with time if I just didn't smoke, I could live with it."

A few weeks later, she considered the issue again. "All right," she told herself, "maybe I will take a flyer on quitting one more time. I'll do it differently this time, however. Instead of regarding each sign of discomfort as a separate catastrophe, and feeling sorry for myself, I'll see them as part of a simple physical withdrawal syndrome which will go away with time, by itself. And rather than making promises to myself and everybody else about how this is the last cigarette I'll ever have, I'll just tell myself that I won't have one *today*.

"And whenever I start to feel deprived because I can't have a cigarette after dinner, I'll say to myself: Gee, you poor baby! You aren't going to get lung cancer! What a pity!"

When the fateful day came, she looked upward

and prayed for the first time in years. Here was her prayer.

"OK, God, if you give me the strength to handle this, I won't give in *today.*"

She swears that to her surprise, quitting smoking on that next attempt was an absolute breeze. That was five years ago.

We think this little story illustrates the difference between *wanting* to change, and being *ready to accept* change.

And we think the same truth applies to an alcoholic who, having given up drinking for the thousandth time, wants desperately to make this a permanent condition.

His or her chances for success depend not only on the desire for change, but also on the willingness *to accept what happens when change occurs.*

◆

When alcoholics first self-diagnose, and quit drinking, we say they are *in compliance.*

They know what alcohol has done to them, and they want that deteriorative process to stop. They have joined AA and begun to work these Steps in the hope that they will help them learn to live without alcohol.

In other words, they have followed directions.

In most cases, these directions come from external sources. It does not feel entirely natural to alcoholics to live sober. They do it because they believe it necessary, and because they are afraid of the alternative. But it is strange to them.

Somewhere in the course of time, at a slightly different point for each person, this attitude changes: you accept the new lifestyle you have chosen.

Rather than stemming from the advice of others, sobriety becomes the product of your own desires. It is now an *internal* program you follow. Not drinking — once a constantly debated issue — becomes as natural as getting up in the morning.

Instead of fighting with yourself over whether or not to attend a certain quota of AA meetings, you now *want* to go. They are rewarding for you.

It's this process — the transition from compliance to acceptance — which the Sixth and Seventh Steps facilitate.

◆

Usually, when someone finds out he suffers from an incurable disease, he experiences a sudden dose of humility. Whatever normally occupies his thoughts — money, sex, glory, failure or success — fades in importance. Any other problems he had now seem trivial, unworthy of attention.

Some people report that in this situation, time itself seems to stop for a moment — as though something which can threaten *your* life threatens the very existence of the world.

Even as a course of treatment is undertaken, and

everyday life goes on, victims of such illnesses claim a new awareness of the relative unimportance of mundane concerns and their egocentric ambitions in the face of this demonstration of their own mortality.

This is entirely understandable. We humans spend much of our lives talking about the importance of good health, but we really learn what health means when we *don't* have it.

"If you have your health, you have everything you need," our grandmothers taught us. But we never acted as though that were true. We wanted more than just to be alive.

That is, until we faced the possibility of death. At that point, "the important things in life" changed: from getting that promotion, buying a new car, showing up your competition, to simpler things—like being able to go get a pizza with your best friend, going out to the ballgame on a summer afternoon, having that familiar face next to you in bed, for one more morning.

People who have heart attacks get a sense of this. Cancer patients understand it. Having incurable, life-threatening illnesses teaches us that life, instead of being our *right,* is really something of a *privilege.*

A privilege which is very often abused.

When an alcoholic first begins treating his or her disease, it is usually from the narrowest of perspectives. The idea that these years of problems with alcohol—so carefully blamed on circumstances, other people, psychological disorders, and the like—could actually represent the progression of a potentially fatal illness, is foreign. Instead, the alcoholic worries about how to turn down drinks at parties, what AA meetings to attend, what to do when faced with a conflict. Which is natural: recovery depends on these daily transitions from the drinking to the non-drinking lifestyle.

Down the road a bit, however, the alcoholic might stop to think about what precisely this process of recovery means.

Perhaps, with clearer brains, lowered defenses, and greater awareness, alcoholics see for the first time how really damaged they were from the effects of this disease.

They might even realize, as so many do, that instead of having had a "couple of years of excessive drinking," they had suffered from alcoholism since adolescence.

Whatever the circumstances, alcoholics usually don't realize the significance of recovery until long after they quit drinking. And sometimes, sitting alone or at an AA meeting, it will hit them like the proverbial ton of bricks.

That "little drinking problem" was a matter of life and death.

Without sobriety, they might not have been here today. By calling on AA and the Higher Power, they had saved their own lives.

This may turn them into "grateful alcoholics" —those who realized, through the experience of recovery, how life really works.

Without the disease, they believe, they might

have spent their days chasing phantasms of success and glory, missing all that really matters. The important parts of life, they have learned, do not center around ambition, pride, or greed.

They have learned humility.

And that is one of the lessons of the Twelve Steps.

Chapter **8**

PICKING UP THE PIECES

◆ ◆ ◆

STEP EIGHT   *Made a list of all persons we
had harmed, and became willing to make
amends to them all.*

Most chronic diseases affect not only their victims, but those close to the victims as well.

In this respect, alcoholism is the undisputed champion. This disease does both direct and indirect damage to people who live with or become involved with the alcoholic. *Direct* damage may be both physical and psychological. *Indirect* damage springs from the misinterpretation of symptoms by those around the alcoholic.

Consider this example. An alcoholic, undiagnosed, goes out with his friends for a beer after work. He plans to spend an hour at the bar and then go home to his family to celebrate his child's birthday.

Once he has a few drinks, however, "home" becomes progressively less important, until he forgets entirely what is supposed to occur. He drinks till about ten o'clock that evening, and then staggers home.

His wife, enraged, yells at him the minute he walks in the door. He knows he's done something wrong, but his befogged brain can't grasp what it is. With nothing better to do, he starts picking on his son for not putting away his things. The child, already angry at his father for spoiling the birthday party, argues back. His father boxes him about the ears, and the boy runs crying to bed. His wife locks the door to the bedroom that night, and the alcoholic sleeps on the couch, with the aid of a few more hits of brandy.

The next day, his child and his wife are furious with him. He can see their anger, but he doesn't know if it has anything to do with him. He doesn't really recall the previous evening.

There are various levels of damage done to the family in this example.

First of all, there's direct, physical damage: a bruised kid. It might as easily have been the wife.

Then, there is direct emotional damage: the wife's faith in her husband's word undermined by his broken promise, her feelings and her child's hurt by her husband's neglect, the boy victimized by his father's displaced anger.

Then, there is considerable indirect damage. Perplexed by her husband's behavior, the wife asks herself, "What's wrong with him lately?" If she's typical, she concludes he is either irresponsible by nature; doesn't care about his family; wanted to punish her for some unknown offense; dislikes his child; or doesn't love her.

The alcoholic's son, on the other hand, concludes that "what's wrong with Dad" is that his father either has been deeply disappointed by his son, is an impossibly mean SOB, or never loved him in the first place.

Above all, the family will be puzzled by the alcoholic's attitude toward them following such an event. "He acts like nothing happened," they'll say to each other. "Maybe the whole thing was just a mistake, or he'd had a hard day at the office, or something." They might work overtime to please him, and be doubly frustrated when, despite their efforts, a similar incident occurs.

They'll become obsessed not only with his strange behavior, his dangerous outbursts, and his moody silence, but with his sheer unpredictability.

The family's preoccupation becomes: "What will happen when Dad comes home *tonight?*

All of the above represents an understandable, inevitable, and completely destructive misinterpretation of events.

After a while, the alcoholic becomes aware of the family's increasingly wary, negative reaction to him. He resorts to defense mechanisms to explain this to himself.

He makes such episodes palatable by telling himself a version of events less damning to himself. He blames other people, including those that he hurts. He denies the occurrence of these episodes, convincing himself of others' craziness. He withdraws and isolates himself. He explodes at the slightest criticism, or refuses to discuss the issue entirely. Above all, he blots this stuff out with more alcohol.

Thus a vicious circle is established. Each symptom of loss of control is complicated by a reaction from others, followed by a counter-reaction from the alcoholic. Layers of misconception and misunderstanding pile upon each other. As a result, whenever the seriousness of these symptoms intrude into the alcoholic's awareness— for example, when he gets a drunk-driving ticket, or a warning from his boss about missing Mondays— instead of being pushed toward correcting the problem, he's pushed toward *more drinking*. This is like adding gasoline to a flame. He treats the results of alcoholic drinking with the cause.

After a few years of this, the alcoholic, whether or not he realizes it, may be laden with guilt. And this guilt may have become as much a part of the problem as the disease itself, since he continues to drink over his own remorse.

Thus, the importance of the Eighth Step. It is nothing more or less than a specific remedy for guilt stemming from your actions while drinking—and it is an alternative to depression and to continued drinking.

This alternative consists of *making amends*. It is designed to repair old wounds and to permit the alcoholic to, in good conscience, set aside the failures of the past, and focus attention fully on the demands of the present.

As we have seen before, change involves not one

action, but two. The first, as before, is the *assumption of willingness*.

Here is how you do the Eighth Step.

First, sit down and make a list of people you believe you have harmed during your drinking.

You'll know who they are. You need not look for everyone you ever insulted, every bill you paid late—those are not what this Step is intended to address. Instead, look at the harm alcoholism did to those who count in your life.

If you feel bad about having done something, then put it on your list. Don't run from the truth.

But above all, while taking this Step, remember that while you did these things you regret, you suffered, unknowingly, from a chronic disease—and from the toxicity, emotional excitement, confusion, and defensiveness that accompany it. These problems resulted not from an evil nature, but from alcoholism. They are as much the effects of this disease as drunkenness, blackouts, and liver damage.

Thus, you should remind yourself that you also suffered from the physical, emotional, and psychological effects of alcoholism, and you may want to make a few amends to yourself as well. The purpose of these Steps is self-honesty, not self-castigation.

How do you know when you are willing to make amends—when the Eighth Step is done?

When you can face the harm your alcoholism did to others, without hating yourself.

Chapter **9**

PUTTING THE
PAST TO REST

◆◆◆

STEP NINE   *Made direct amends to such
people whenever possible, except when to do so
would injure them or others.*

At first glance, the Ninth Step seems one of the simplest and most straightforward of the Twelve.

In the Eighth Step, the alcoholics listed those who had been harmed as a result of their drinking. Step Nine quite logically asks that they proceed to make amends to these persons, in preparation for beginning a life free of drinking. But the question arises as to what constitutes "amends." What, precisely, does an alcoholic have to do to make up for the damage of the past?

For some alcoholics, this presents no problems. But for others, more creative and less logical, the Ninth Step is the stuff from which legends are born.

We knew one fellow who had, on a particular

three-day binge, managed to lose $10,000 in Las Vegas. When he sobered up, he had no recollection of where the money had gone. Had he spent it, gambled it away, been robbed, left it in a restaurant or hotel room, or simply tossed it out the window? There was no way he could find out.

This wasn't the first time this had happened to an alcoholic, and it wouldn't be the last. There was, however, one slight problem complicating this particular situation.

It wasn't the alcoholic's money.

The $10,000 belonged to the alcoholic's boss, and represented the week's receipts from a grocery where the alcoholic worked. The alcoholic was to have deposited it in the bank on his way home from work.

As he came to his senses, the alcoholic realized that not only would he get fired for losing the money, his boss might even believe that he had stolen it. Therefore, he had to invent a robbery to cover his trail.

Putting his brain into overdrive, he developed a plan.

First, he searched the parking lot until, to his unending relief, he found his car. Apparently he hadn't flown to Las Vegas; there would be no ticket records to haunt him. He had no credit cards; there also would be no record to prove he had come to Nevada. So all he had to do was bribe the hotel clerk to destroy his registration card, which he did.

Next, he drove back to his home. In his garage, he

found a hammer. In his medicine cabinet, he found a bottle of barbiturates.

Taking several of the barbiturates and washing them down with whiskey, he waited until he started to get sleepy. Then, before he passed out, he summoned up all his will power and gave himself a solid whack on the side of his head with the hammer.

He slept without interruption until the next morning. Then, he called the police, and when they came, told them the following story:

"I left work about noon on Friday with the money, and got caught in traffic and didn't make it to the bank on time. Well, I knew my boss would be mad, and I was scared I'd get fired, so I decided to take the money home with me and take it to the bank first thing Monday morning.

"So I locked it in my file cabinet and went to bed that night. About three in the morning, I woke up to find my house being burglarized. I tried to get to the telephone, but these two men caught me and knocked me around. I was terrified they were going to kill me. I thought they had come because they knew I had the money, and I told them I'd tell them where it was if they wouldn't kill me. They agreed, and I told them about the cash in the file cabinet. Now I realize they probably didn't know about the $10,000, and I gave it away for no good reason. But at the time, I was sure that's why they had come.

"Anyway, once they had the money, they locked me in the garage. I just this moment managed to get out."

Well, as far-fetched as this story seems, the police and his boss seemed to buy it. The money was insured, and replaced, and the alcoholic was summarily fired. But no criminal charges were brought, and the alcoholic prayed that he had heard the last of this episode.

About a year afterward, this alcoholic joined AA and stopped drinking. Later on, when doing his Ninth Step, he faced a dilemma: Should I or should I not come clean about this episode? Should I try to make amends?

His sponsor counseled him that in a case like this, where restitution has been made to the man whose money was lost, and where rigorous honesty might lead to greater grief for that man as well as for the alcoholic himself, it was wiser to let well enough alone. To undertake to pay back the $10,000 would probably just result in a jail sentence for the alcoholic, and force the boss to pay the money back to the insurance company.

So the alcoholic decided to forget it. He went on with the Steps, telling himself that if a chance to make amends without risking everything arose, he would take it.

Then one day about a year later, a package arrived in the mail, containing a letter and about $3,500 in cash. The letter said:

"Dear Sir: We are the family you helped out with your kind donation years ago in Las Vegas. We want you to know that our little Bobbie is doing just fine. Without your help, he might not have lived.

"You are always in our prayers. We would like to pay back some of the money you gave us, which we never used but which we saved in case Bobbie got sick again. But now that we don't need it, we want to give it back. You told us how rich you were, and we know you don't need it, but it would make us feel better to return it.

"Thank you, and may God bless you."

The alcoholic, obviously, had simply given the money away in a fit of good samaritanism, and forgotten it. He took the package of money, rewrapped it, and mailed it to the insurance company that had paid his boss's claim.

◆

When you do your Ninth Step, it helps to remember the phrase "except when to do so would injure them or others."

Modern translation: "except when making amends does more harm than good."

Suppose that one of the people you feel you need to make amends to is your ex-spouse. You'd like to call and apologize for what you once did.

Your ex has remarried, however, and you're concerned that your call could upset this new relationship. It's probably better to forget it. If hearing from you might do more harm than good, then you shouldn't try.

The purpose of the Ninth Step, then, is to put the past to rest. It should allow you to give up your preoccupation with the way life *used to be* and affirm your new attitude, centered firmly in the way life is *now*.

The ''amends'' of this Step are a way of burning a few emotional bridges—those involving guilt—while building new bridges that depend on honest communication.

10

NO BACKSLIDING

◆ ◆ ◆

STEP TEN *Continued to take personal inventory and when we were wrong promptly admitted it.*

L ike the rest of the human race, we hate to be wrong.

Well, let's qualify that. If the issue in dispute is unimportant, then we don't mind admitting we made a mistake.

We don't particularly *like* it, but it's not all that traumatic.

On the other hand, if the matter in question is something we hold dear—some fondly-held assumption, or cherished belief—when we positively *hate* to have it challenged.

It can even be a mortifying, awful experience.

We don't find ourselves unusual in this respect. All our friends, family, neighbors, acquaintances, and enemies seem to behave the same way.

Since nobody we know likes being wrong, we've come to believe this is human nature. Everybody wants to be right; nobody wants to be wrong.

Nevertheless, with distressing frequency, all of us are.

Take our experience in alcoholism treatment some years ago. At the time, we were using what we regarded as "state-of-the-art" techniques: teaching alcoholics that they suffered from an underlying personality disorder which led to drinking, and which therefore had to be the real focus of treatment. The physical part of alcoholism, we thought, ended when the patient stopped shaking. The really important addiction was psychological. After all, wasn't that why the patient had begun drinking in the first place?

Some time during this period, one of our patients handed us a copy of a monograph by a fellow named James Milam. This hard-to-read essay—printed on the awfulest orange paper you ever saw—challenged every belief we had about alcoholism, in no uncertain terms.

Instead of resulting from personality disorders, alcoholism, according to Milam, was entirely the result of a physical adaptation. It was inheritable, Milam claimed, and the various psychosocial problems that were the focus of treatment as we knew it, were the results, not the cause, of the illness.

Instead of representing permanent character flaws that would dog the alcoholic throughout life, these psychological problems would clear up over time, *if* the alcoholic stopped drinking.

This was revolutionary. So we checked all this research that Milam cited, and found that indeed, alcoholism did appear to be just what he claimed it was

—a chronic physiological disease.

There were continuing arguments among researchers, of course, but this didn't bother us. A scientist friend of ours jokingly defines research in the life sciences as "guesswork followed by debate."

To our eyes, however, the point was clear: alcoholism did not appear to be a mental illness. It did not seem to represent a personality disorder. It was not a response to situational stress, or an effort to self-medicate an underlying emotional problem.

This put us in quite a bind because just about every treatment method we used was based upon those assumptions, now shown to be incorrect.

Our conflict was obvious. We had treated a lot of alcoholics over the years, sending them to AA, helping a lot of them get sober. We'd made some major changes in philosophy along the way, but nothing *this* major.

Suppose we just kept right on teaching what we had always taught? People still got sober, didn't they? Why go through all the trauma of changing our methods? We didn't see any of the other "experts" changing theirs. Who'd know the difference?

We would.

We could keep doing what we were doing. Or we could admit we had been wrong, take a long, hard look at ourselves, and change.

That's what we decided to do. In this instance, our pride in the quality of our work was greater than our need to be right.

It was awkward at first. Everything we had been doing, remember, was based on outdated assumptions. This meant that our patients and their families would keep pointing out inconsistencies in what we were doing now.

One of us recalls a day when he was lecturing to a group on the importance of some form of emotional growth in becoming a self-actualized person. One of the alcoholics in the audience asked him to explain precisely what all this had to do with getting sober.

He rationalized it for the alcoholic, but thought to himself, "You know, that really is a good question. What *does* this have to do with getting sober?"

There went another assumption.

Slowly, through a process of being wrong, having this pointed out, and making changes, we developed a treatment program which was still based on the Steps of AA, but which was also consistent with our new understanding of alcoholism as a disease. It by no means appeared overnight. Our new program grew out of our ongoing examination of ourselves and our methods over the course of years.

Sometimes we made a change in the program we thought would help, and then discovered that it didn't. Then we had to admit we'd been wrong again, and start all over from scratch.

Sometimes we had to swallow our pride, admit that we simply didn't know how to deal with a particular problem, and ask somebody else to show us what *they* did. Then we could copy it.

Out of all this making and correcting mistakes

came what we believe is a consistent, effective, useful, and above all, *workable* program of treatment. We're happy to have it, and we plan to leave it alone. That is, until we find the next mistake.

◆

If you haven't figured it out by now, what we just described represents a sort of Tenth Step.

We identified an error in our approach—a real doozy, it turned out. We swallowed our pride, our need to be right, and began to rework our methods.

This had to be done on a daily basis. There was no way we could have foreseen the changes we would have to make before the program began to work. We had to be *flexible*. Had we insisted on doing only those few things we had originally planned on, our "reconstruction" of attitude and approach would have been a complete failure. We had to have a method for making changes *as we went along*.

This is the spirit of the Tenth Step. You solidify and improve your Program through *continual* self-examination. That way, you can overcome your worst enemy in recovery: your own very natural, human, need to be right.

Your Program of recovery can change as you change—can come alive, as it were, as you do.

By taking the time to look at what you're doing every day, you can see solutions to problems you never could have identified in a Fourth Step.

Chapter 11

STAYING ON THE PATH

◆◆◆

STEP ELEVEN *Sought through prayer and meditation to improve our conscious contact with God* as we understood Him, *praying only for knowledge of His will for us and the power to carry that out.*

When you ask a drinking alcoholic what's wrong with his life, he *looks outside himself* for the answer.

He's not getting promoted fast enough at work. He's married to a nag. His kids are delinquents. The tax people want too much money. His house is too small.

When you ask him what he believes would improve the quality of his life, he once again looks at making external changes.

Maybe he should get a divorce, find a woman who really understands him. Maybe he should switch careers, or move to a new neighborhood.

This lifelong habit of *externalization* helps to blind him to his own predicament with alcohol.

Drinking, from his viewpoint, is the medicine

which makes this external unpleasantness tolerable. Without alcohol, he couldn't cope.

He drinks too much, he believes, because his life is so difficult.

For most alcoholics, recovery involves an almost total reversal of this attitude. Instead of looking outside themselves for the sources of their problems, they learn to look at their own behavior, their own attitudes. And instead of seeking solutions in superficial changes of environment, recovering alcoholics are told to seek help through contact with a Higher Power.

At first, asking an alcoholic to look inward is like asking a duck to fly backward. It can be done, but only for short periods.

As time passes, however, it gets easier, for several reasons.

First, the alcoholic's brain begins to clear. Thinking, judgement, and emotional control all improve, just because they are no longer being attacked with alcohol.

Second, abstinence brings a halt to many of the psychosocial problems that alcoholic drinking causes. It's easier to deal with the last drunk-driving arrest because there won't be another one. Problems stop piling up.

Third, the reality—hard as it is for the alcoholic to believe at first—is that a large portion of the dissatisfaction with life was the product of the alcoholic's own attitude. Life was never that awful in the first place, except where drinking made it so.

One woman we know told us about her experience with her sponsor in AA. Whenever she went to her sponsor with a problem, she would get the same response.

The sponsor would tell her, "It is a spiritual truth that the solution to all our problems lies within ourselves." That's all she'd say. No discussion, no argument.

"Wait a minute," our friend would yell. "I've got a lousy marriage on my hands. I've got my boss on my tail. I need practical advice, not Oriental wisdom. Tell me what I should do about this problem."

In answer, her sponsor would smile benignly.

"It is a spiritual truth . . . " she would begin.

"I know, I know," our friend would respond. "Just forget I asked, OK?"

After about a year of this—marked by many problems, followed by the same advice—our friend finally experienced the proverbial flash of understanding.

She'd just gone through her usual process of solving a problem—which for her always involved much worry and manipulation of people and events—when it struck her: "Hey," she said to herself, "I really knew what I had to do right from the beginning. Why didn't I just go ahead and *do* it? Why did I put myself through all that grief first?"

Then a second insight occurred to her.

"Maybe that's my problem," she thought. "I make mountains out of molehills. I don't take life as it is. I'm always setting myself up to be disappointed in people.

"Maybe," she continued, "that's why I'm so dissatisfied with life all the time. Maybe *I'm* the problem—what I expect, how I approach things—not life."

She began to act as if this might be the case. She began to act as if the solution to problems lay within herself. And as it turned out, many of them did. She knew this was true because her life began to improve, almost immediately.

It felt almost like the end of a long-standing war between that alcoholic and her own life.

This illustrates an important point about the Eleventh Step. The answer, if you will, to that alcoholic's problems lay right in front of her all along. In fact, her sponsor went so far as to repeat it over and over, in the simplest possible terms, every time the alcoholic brought her a problem.

In the Eleventh Step, the recovering alcoholic is advised to seek, through prayer and meditation, to maintain conscious contact with his or her Higher Power. This is because the new-found HP cannot help you unless you make yourself available to it.

That involves a form of "active listening" which, the Step implies, is best done through meditation and prayer.

For many alcoholics, the Eleventh Step also involves another long-neglected aspect of recovery: improving the *quality* of life. That doesn't generally refer to making more money, getting a better-looking mate, or any of that sort of "improvement." It does mean doing things which make life more meaningful and satisfying to you.

Things such as being of service to other people.

Or getting healthy.

Or learning new skills.

Remember, it's *quality* that counts, not *quantity*. It doesn't matter how *much* you have, but rather how *satisfying* it is.

The reason for this should be obvious: if your life is satisfying to you—and you have learned to be satisfied with yourself, as well as with those around you—you'll be that much less likely to relapse.

Just don't forget: It is a spiritual truth that the solutions to most problems lie within ourselves.

Chapter 12

THE MESSAGE

◆ ◆ ◆

STEP TWELVE   *Having had a spiritual awakening as a result of these steps, we tried to carry this message to alcoholics, and to practice these principles in all our affairs.*

There's an old story in AA about the newcomer who approached his sponsor for help in understanding the Twelfth Step.

"I get the part about carrying the message and practicing the principles," the newcomer explained. "But I can't say I've had a 'spiritual awakening.' I mean, that sounds like God talks to you or there's a sign from Heaven, and nothing like that has ever happened to me in my life!"

"Look," his sponsor told him. "Six months ago, your life was a complete mess, right?"

"Right," the newcomer agreed.

"And you were about to lose your job, and your wife was seeing a lawyer, and the judge was getting ready to sentence you to ninety days for drunk driving, wasn't he?"

"Yes, that's all true," the newcomer said.

77

"And then you joined AA," continued his sponsor, "stopped drinking, and all that stuff began to clear up, right?"

"It sure did."

"All right then," the sponsor concluded. "For a drunk like you, that's a spiritual awakening."

◆

Look at what happens in the life of an alcoholic who finally reaches the stage we call "sobriety."

BEFORE	NOW
Usually intoxicated	Sober
Often sick	Usually feels good
Angry, hostile, depressed	Calmer, less defensive
Poor judgement	Makes decisions rationally
Lots of personal conflict	Gets along better with others
Tries to change everyone else	Learning to change self
Hardly ever content	Sometimes actually happy!
Medically in danger	Getting healthy

OK, so maybe there wasn't any sign from God. But the above will have to do.

The problem in treating alcoholism—as with any chronic, incurable illness—lies not in initiating recovery, but in *maintaining* it. The Twelfth Step suggests that the best way to learn is to teach.

And who better to teach than others who have this

same illness? Who needs the benefit of your knowledge and experience more than they? Thus the idea
of "carrying the message" was born, and became
part of the fabric of AA.

Some AA historians believe that Bill Wilson's
greatest contribution to the birth of AA was his realization that if one alcoholic devoted time and energy
to helping another stay sober, then that "helper"
would be successful even if the "helpee" got drunk
—since he himself had been able to make it through
another day without alcohol. It was a simple, yet
profound insight.

By carrying the message of sobriety to others, the
alcoholic also carried it to himself.

In that respect, the Twelfth Step is curiously
linked with the First. In reaching out to the suffering
alcoholic, the AA member confronts his or her own
memory of powerlessness and unmanageability and
is forced to recall the painful circumstances which
brought him or her to AA in the first place.

This is crucial, because it is human nature to
forget an unpleasant experience as soon as we can.

Imagine yourself withdrawing from alcohol in a
detox ward. You may be wracked with tremors so
severe you can't lift a cup of coffee. Your stomach
feels like it wants to leap up your throat. Every mus-
cle in your body aches. You can hardly walk to the
bathroom.

In the midst of this misery, you make yourself a
promise. "I'll never forget *this*," you vow. "I'll
never forget how bad I feel now. When I go to drink,

this memory will stop me."

Three months later, fit again, you sit at the bar next to an old friend and consider the drink you have just ordered.

"Don't you think you better skip that?" your friend asks. "Remember what you said when they let you out of the hospital."

"Yes, I know," you answer. "But I've been off it for quite a while now, and I'm not sick like I was then. Besides, I wasn't ever that bad. I wasn't really hooked on the stuff."

Another three months pass, and despite all your efforts, you find yourself back in the hospital, making the same vows to yourself.

This is the paradox of alcoholism—and also of chronic illnesses like heart disease, diabetes, and emphysema.

When they are *in control*—the alcoholic is sober, the diabetic on insulin, the heart patient on medication, the emphysemic breathing well—it is difficult to recall how it was when they were *not in control*.

The Twelve Step Program makes provision for this phenomenon, by suggesting that you remind yourself of the severity of your illness through the simple medium of reminding others.

◆

Actually, the hardest part of the Twelve Steps comes in the last words of the final Step.

They are: " . . . and to practice these principles in

all our affairs."

In other words, to use the ideas set forth in the Steps not only in regard to alcoholism, *but in everything you do*.

This reflects the actual origin of the AA Step Program, which was adapted from that of the Oxford Movement. This was a group of people from all walks of life who set out to live in a better, more satisfying fashion.

They didn't have the wreckage of alcoholic drinking to motivate them. They just wanted to be better people.

Indeed, the Steps can be applied to almost any aspect of living, by looking at the concepts which underlie each Step:

STEP ONE

I recognize that there exist great portions of life—such as disease, death, and the behavior of other people—over which I have no control. When I try to control that which I cannot, I make my life unmanageable, and myself miserable.

STEP TWO

As painful as it may be to admit, I need someone or something outside myself, to show me how to live better, and to give me the strength to change.

STEP THREE

Now that I have found something to act as a Higher Power, I will do my best to surrender to it, rather than continuing to rely exclusively on my own will.

STEP FOUR

In preparation for changing the way I live, I will take an honest look at my own strengths and weaknesses so that I can base my actions on a foundation of self-knowledge.

STEP FIVE

Rather than pretending to others that I have no weaknesses, I will share what I have learned about myself with those I care about.

STEP SIX

I will adopt a posture of *readiness* for the changes I seek. I accept the need for changes in my attitudes and beliefs if I am to live a more satisfying life.

STEP SEVEN

I will set about changing my attitudes, values, and behavior, asking for the guidance of my Higher Power and of others whom I trust.

STEP EIGHT

I acknowledge that my behavior may have hurt others besides myself and have decided that I will try to set things right.

STEP NINE

I will make amends wherever possible, unless it

would do more harm than good.

STEP TEN

I will keep a close watch on my thinking for attitudes which might threaten my health and happiness, and make no attempt to hide my difficulties from those who could help me.

STEP ELEVEN

I will attempt, in every way possible, to improve the *quality* of my life, so that it might be fuller, happier, and more productive.

STEP TWELVE

As I learn to accept my self and others, I will try to carry this knowledge to those who need it, and to bring my new outlook to every aspect of my life.

We know psychologists who would call this a blueprint for mental health.

It's helpful to remember, therefore, that the Steps aren't there only to help you *quit* drinking. They can also help you *live without* drinking. Which some people don't realize.

One psychoanalyst we know sent us a patient for consultation. This fellow had been in therapy for five years, and had quit drinking a year ago for the usual reasons—threat of divorce, loss of job, and such. He'd attended AA for three months when he first quit drinking, but dropped out as soon as he lost the craving for alcohol. Unfortunately, he still suffered from an almost constant sense of frustration and dissatisfaction with life, and especially with his own position in it.

We suggested he return to AA.

"What for?" he responded. "I quit drinking. Why go to AA if I'm not drinking?"

"Did you notice a lot of other people at those meetings?" we asked him.

"Yes," he said.

"Were any of *them* drinking?"

"No," he admitted.

"Then why do you think *they* go to meetings?"

We left him pondering that.

◆

Despite the fact that so many alcoholics join AA and get well, there still exists a tendency among some observers to notice only those who *fail* to recover.

It is this phenomenon—in combination with the misconception that alcoholism is somehow *not* a disease—that has given the alcoholic an unfair stigma among victims of chronic diseases.

The fact is that from a clinical standpoint, alcoholism is no more difficult to treat than diabetes, emphysema, or heart disease, and the relapse rate among alcoholics may actually be lower than among victims of these other illnesses.

We suspect that some day we will see the principles and structure of AA, including the Twelve Step

Program, adapted to the treatment of such diseases. We can easily see how a "self-help fellowship" for heart patients could be of enormous benefit not only to victims of that disease, but to the physicians who treat them.

The problem that faces medicine is clear, and it is as old as the hills. Where we cannot cure a disease, our only hope lies in teaching the patient to live with it to the very best of his or her ability.

The medical term for this is "patient compliance," as in "the prognosis is good, depending on patient compliance with the treatment."

This is the aspect of chronic disease medicine that we can't control.

Yes, the drug will help, *if the patient takes it*.

Yes, the exercises will improve breathing, *if the patient does them*.

Yes, lowered stress and continued exercise will decrease the chances for another heart attack, *providing the patient does not return to previous activities*.

In the past, physicians have been able to do little more than advise their patients what they must do, and warn them of the consequences if they fail to follow directions.

Sometimes this works, but more often, it doesn't. That's why a lot of people have second heart attacks. That's why a lot of alcoholics drink again.

Left to our own devices, we tend to do what we have always done.

It's almost as though there exists a kind of

"lifestyle inertia," which fights us when we need to change. It seems to want us to go in the same direction we've been going, *even if it kills us*.

AA found that what alcoholics could not do by themselves, could be done when they worked together. A disease which resisted all efforts of individual will, could in fact be controlled within the structure of a fellowship and its simple program for recovery.

It worked. It grew into what we know as the Twelve Steps.

And that, more than anything else, is AA's gift to humanity.

SUGGESTED READING
♦ ♦ ♦

Recently we selected at random five popular books on alcoholism from the shelves of our favorite bookstore and checked each to see how alcoholism was defined. Of the five, four stated that alcoholism was *not* a disease.

Obviously, it is still easy to be misinformed about the illness.

The following list, although brief, provides the names of books that offer sound information regarding alcoholism and its treatment.

ALCOHOLISM

Under the Influence: A Guide to the Myths and Realities of Alcoholism. James R. Milam and Katherine Ketcham, New York, Bantam Books, 1983.

The best description—bar none—of alcoholism as a chronic, hereditary, physiological disease. Milam's model forms the basis for our approach.

HELP FOR THE FAMILY

Getting Them Sober (Parts 1 and 2). Toby Rice Drews, Plainfield, NJ, Bridge Publishing, 1980.

Simple, Al-Anon-influenced advice for family members faced with the task of living with a drinking or sober alcoholic.

INTERVENTION

I'll Quit Tomorrow. Vernon Johnson, New York, Harper & Row, 1980.

The first real description of the process of structured intervention with alcoholics. Some of the book is outdated but it is still of interest to families and friends as well as professionals.

Intervention: How to Help Someone Who Doesn't Want Help. Vernon Johnson, Minneapolis, Johnson Institute, 1986.

A practical guide to the process of intervention; more detailed than *I'll Quit Tomorrow*, with examples of family confrontation.

PUBLICATIONS OF ALCOHOLICS ANONYMOUS (NEW YORK, AA WORLD SERVICES)

Alcoholics Anonymous (often known as "The Big Book"). Bill W., 1955.

AA's bible. Early AA members came from all walks of life, and their stories of addiction and recovery form the backbone of this book, as an illustration of AA's strength: the ability to discover and make use of *common experience* as the basis for recovery.

Twelve Steps and Twelve Traditions. Bill W., 1953.

An explanation of the Twelve Steps that includes suggestions for working the AA program.

Living Sober. 1975.

An unimposing little book that nonetheless is a helpful guide to the first weeks and months without alcohol.

RECOVERY

Eating Right to Live Sober. L. Ann Mueller, M.D., and Katherine Ketcham, New York, New American Library, 1985.

A guide to nutrition and diet specifically for those recovering from alcoholism.

Recovering: How to Get and Stay Sober. L. Ann Mueller, M.D., and Katherine Ketcham, New York, Bantam, 1987.

General information about the treatment and recovery process. The book offers a good description of alcoholic behavior and is soundly based on James Milam's Chronic Disease Model.

TREATMENT FOR THE ALCOHOLIC

Don't Help: A Guide to Working with the Alcoholic. Ronald L. Rogers and Chandler Scott McMillan, New York, Bantam Books, 1989.

A book written in informal language for helpers—be they family, friends, or health-care professionals. Based on James Milam's Chronic Disease Model, the book explains outdated and current views of the disease; how treatment and recovery work; and what helpers should do and should avoid.

NOTES

NOTES

NOTES

ABOUT THE AUTHORS

RONALD L. ROGERS and CHANDLER SCOTT MCMILLIN each directs an addiction treatment center, and both are members of the adjunct faculty of the University of Virgina. MORRIS A. HILL is a former member of the Maryland Alcoholism Counselor Certification Board and a consultant to two addiction treatment centers.

BANTAM BOOKS ON
ADDICTION AND RECOVERY

ADDICTION

The most up-to-date information from the leading experts in the field.

800-COCAINE
Mark S. Gold, M.D.
From the leading expert on cocaine abuse and treatment, an informative, prescriptive manual with hard facts on America's fastest-growing drug problem.
34388-2   *Large Format Paperback* $3.50/$3.95 in Canada

THE FACTS ABOUT DRUGS AND ALCOHOL
Mark S. Gold, M.D.
The bestselling author of **800-COCAINE** provides concise, medically-proven information on marijuana, heroin, LSD, crack, and other commonly abused substances.
27826-6   *Paperback* $3.95/$4.95 in Canada

UNDER THE INFLUENCE
A Guide to the Myths and Realities of Alcoholism
James R. Milam, Ph.D., and Katherine Ketcham
This groundbreaking classic emphasizes treating alcoholism as a physiological disease and offers information on how to tell if someone is an alcoholic, treatment, and recovery.
27487-2   *Paperback* $4.95/$5.95 in Canada

SEX, DRUGS & AIDS
Oralee Wachter
For every family—offers advice and dispels dangerous myths about AIDS, by the author of *No More Secrets for Me*.
34454-4   *Large Format Paperback* $3.95/$4.95 in Canada

RECOVERY

From alcoholism to eating disorders, books that offer concrete tools for physical, emotional, and spiritual recovery.

LIVING ON THE EDGE
A Guide to Intervention for Families with Drug and Alcohol Problems
Katherine Ketcham and Ginny Lyford Gustafson
From two reknowned professionals, compassionate, step-by-step advice on every facet of family intervention, from preparation to finding the right treatment options and support groups.
34606-7   *Large Format Paperback* $7.95/$9.95 in Canada

EATING WITHOUT FEAR
A Guide to Understanding and Overcoming Bulimia
Leigh Cohn and Lindsey Hall
Warm and supportive, this book helps the reader set realistic goals and discusses support systems as well as how to establish healthier eating habits. Includes a Two-week "Stop-binging" Program and advice for family and friends.
28377-4   *Paperback* $3.95/$4.95 in Canada

RECOVERING
How to Get and Stay Sober
L. Ann Mueller, M.D., and Katherine Ketcham
An essential resource for alcoholics and those who love them, a comprehensive and compassionate guide to new treatment programs that have helped many alcoholics achieve lasting sobriety.
34303-3   *Large Format Paperback* $8.95/$11.95 in Canada

RECLAIMING OUR LIVES
Hope for Adult Survivors of Incest
Carol Poston and Karen Lison
A comprehensive, inspiring, and supportive guide with a concrete, 14-step program for healing written by an incest survivor and a therapist.
28497-5   *Paperback* $4.95/$5.95 in Canada

DON'T HELP
A Positive Guide to Working with the Alcoholic
Ronald L. Rogers and Chandler Scott McMillin
For counselors, health-care professionals, and families a definitive and practical guide to working with the alcoholic.
34716-0   *Large Format Paperback* $8.95/$11.95 in Canada

<u>ADULT CHILDREN</u>
Essential reading for the millions who grew up in dysfunctional families.

THE ADULT CHILDREN OF ALCOHOLICS SYNDROME
Wayne Kritsberg
Real help and hope for adult children in a complete self-help program that shows how to recognize and remedy the effects of the dysfunctional family.
27279-9   *Paperback* $3.95/$4.95 in Canada

BECOMING YOUR OWN PARENT
The Solution for Adult Children of Alcoholic and Other Dysfunctional Families
Dennis Wholey
Television host Dennis Wholey, author of *The Courage to Change* and himself an "adult child," takes us inside a series of meetings where

fourteen men and women learn to find within themselves the validation and nurturance they were denied as children. Also offers the wisdom of a dozen nationally recognized experts on recovery.
34788-8   *Large Format Paperback* $8.95/$11.95 in Canada

HEALING FOR ADULT CHIILDREN OF ALCOHOLICS
Sara Hines Martin
A groundbreaking work that examines the spiritual and emotional healing that must take place for complete recovery from the ACOA Syndrome. "Truly commendable." —Dr. Robert H. Schuller
28246-8   *Paperback* $4.50/$5.50 in Canada

POTATO CHIPS FOR BREAKFAST
The True Story of Growing Up in an Alcoholic Family
Cynthia Scales
The shocking true story of a young girl who grew up with every material comfort—and two alcoholic parents.
28166-6   *Paperback* $3.50/$4.50 in Canada

FAMILY ISSUES
Groundbreaking books on conquering co-dependence and helping addicted family members.

LOVING AN ALCOHOLIC
Help and Hope for Co-dependents
Jack Mumey
The founder of the Gateway Treatment Center for alcoholics and their families presents practical advice—a way out of confusion and pain, and past roadblocks to change.
27326-5   *Paperback* $4.50/$5.50 in Canada

ADDICTED TO ADULTERY
How We Saved Our Marriage
How You Can Save Yours
Richard and Elizabeth Brzeczek and Sharon De Vita
The former Chicago police superintendent and his wife discuss how infidelity nearly destroyed their marriage, and how they formed WESOM (We Saved Our Marriage), the first self-help group for married couples devastated by adultery, featuring the 12-step Relationship Recovery Program.
05397-3   *Hardcover* $17.95/$21.95 in Canada

TOXIC PARENTS
Overcoming their Hurtful Legacy and Reclaiming Your Life
Dr. Susan Forward with Craig Buck
The challenging, compassionate, and controversial new guide to recognizing and recovering from the lasting damage caused by physical or emotional abuse in childhood, by the bestselling author of *Men Who Hate Women & the Women Who Love Them*.
05700-6   *Hardcover* $18.95/$23.95 in Canada

HEALING RELATIONSHIPS

Books that point readers toward a healthier self and new ways of relating with others.

HOW TO BREAK YOUR ADDICTION TO A PERSON
Howard M. Halpern, Ph.D.
An insightful, step-by-step guide to breaking painful addictive relationships—and surviving separation.
26005-7   *Paperback* $4.50/$4.95 in Canada

OUT OF DARKNESS INTO THE LIGHT
A Journey of Inner Healing
Gerald G. Jampolsky, M.D.
The bestselling author of *Love is Letting Go of Fear* offers a blueprint for recovery through his personal journey from severe depression, guilt, and alcohol abuse to a triumphant rediscovery of self and inner healing.
05350-7   *Hardcover* $14.95/$18.95 in Canada

BECOMING NATURALLY THERAPEUTIC
A Return to the True Essence of Helping
Jacquelyn Small
The renown workshop leader's inspiring guide for all who serve as listeners or counselors in the lives of others. Basing her work on landmark studies, Small helps us "straight-talk" beyond our co-dependent or controlling ways of helping others and teaches how to offer clear and loving guidance directly from the heart.
34800-0   *Large Format Paperback* $7.95/$9.95 in Canada

MEDITATIONALS

Daily inspiration and guidance based on the 12-step programs.

A NEW DAY
365 Meditations for Personal and Spiritual Growth
Anonymous
Offers spiritual and psychological guidance on overcoming the struggles we face each day, by the author of *A Day at a Time.*
34591-5   *Paperback* $6.95/$8.95 in Canada

FAMILY FEELINGS
Daily Meditations for Healthy Relationships
Martha Vanceburg and Sylvia Silverman
Valuable insights on changing destructive family patterns with one's spouse, children, elderly parents, and grandparents. By the coauthor of *The Promise of a New Day* and her mother.
34705-5   *Paperback* $6.95/$8.95 in Canada

Prices subject to change.